fated
to
break

thoughts on heartbreak
by olive rhodes

Copyright © 2022 Olive Rhodes

ISBN: 9798360488095

if loving you was fate
then this pain is too

i know i'm destined for something
much greater than you

if there was a spokesperson
for rose-colored glasses
it would be me

i couldn't see
your red flags
if my life depended on it

we were made up of
late night drives
and hungry kisses
2 am phone calls
and flimsy promises

everything about us
was rushed and fragile
the foundation was
cracked at best
but i would have lived there
my whole life

come with me
you said

of course
i replied
i'll follow you
anywhere

i loved how
you made me feel
like i was desirable
like you couldn't get
enough of me

-the feeling was mutual

you worshipped me, or at least that's what it felt like. my skin against your skin became my religion. your body became my altar, and mine became yours. i would have parted the sea to taste you. hell, i would have simply drowned in it to get an extra minute with your mouth on mine.

-drowning in desire

you never hesitated
to show me that
you wanted me

it was just
the love part
that was missing

-love and lust aren't the same

the thing is that i didn't feel like i was lovable before you.
and that makes it all the more terrible that you tricked me
the way you did. because i had been waiting for so long
for somebody to make me feel this way, and i thought
with you, i'd found it.

if you take
one thing from my story
let it be to not fall
for the boys with
silver tongues
and silken promises

-it's all a trap

i'm just not ready for a relationship
you kept saying that

but then
you'd stay weekends at my place
you'd take me out to dinner
you'd cook me breakfast
you'd even bring me flowers (twice)

you did all these things
that screamed *relationship*
for months

all these things
except
commitment

it all seemed so real
i fell for it
hook
line and sinker

the saying
if they wanted to they would
exists for a reason

and it's not always so black and white
people have histories and scars
traumas and fears

but when it came to *this*
to simply cementing
what we had
into something more legitimate

i know now
that there was no excuse
no ex that made you scared
or something like that

it was simply
if you had wanted to
you would have

and you just
didn't

you were wrong for me
in so many ways
but i never found it in me to care
i was too addicted to the way
your lips felt on mine to notice
they were laced with poison

-*deliciously toxic*

when i realized
i was in love with you
i felt fucking sick
that probably should
have been my
warning sign

loving you was
the sweetest
downfall

so beautiful
i didn't even notice
the ground rising
up to meet me
until it was
too late

nothing hurt more
than that crash landing
when i realized
i had been the only one

f
a
l
l
i
n
g

i never said
that i loved you.
i knew you'd run
if i did.

well,
you ran anyway.

now i'm stuck
with these words
i never got to say.

when you said
i was easy to be with
i thought that meant
i was easy to love
not easy to use and discard

-my mistake

i wanted you so badly
i would have done anything—
would've turned my back on fate,
would've laughed in the face of destiny.

anything to ignore what was coming.

when we hit three months
and you still wouldn't make it official
i should have known
i was just being used

and maybe i did know
somewhere deep inside me
i just didn't want to accept it

if i was so

beautiful
sexy
fun
sweet
smart
funny
perfect

why didn't
you want
to make us
into something

real?

-mixed signals

maybe it was just
the hopeless romantic in me
but by the end of it
i had really started to believe
in us

what if
i told you
that i always knew
we were doomed
from the start?

i thought
we'd beaten the odds.

when five months had passed
and you were still here,
i thought
we'd beaten the odds.

but i guess i got too comfortable.
i guess i let my guard down.

because the moment
i began to see you as
anything close to permanent,
you left.

but i just thought
we'd beaten the odds.

everyone told me
to stay away from you

said you were trouble
that you'd chew me up
and spit me out

but you said i was different

god
i thought i was different

we were a clock
counting down

i always knew
there was only
so much time
before you got
tired of me

i just wish
it had taken
a bit longer
before we reached

zero

do you remember
that october night
when you looked at me
like i was the only person
in the room?

we were surrounded
by people but it didn't matter.

in that moment,
none of it mattered.

-take me back there

god,
i thought you loved
me too.

was that so bad?

-you fooled me

you started kissing me in public
what else was i supposed to do
but read into that?

i could've sworn
you almost said it once
when we were
half drunk
and barely clothed
you stared at me
through drooping eyelids
with a lopsided smile
and i could've sworn
i saw the words
sitting right there
fighting against your lips
to be let out

-i love you

i knew from the moment
you said my name
that you'd ruin me

i don't think i left
your name half as bloody

-you never gave me the same power

i was
so easy
to trap.

all it took
was one pretty smile
and a flash of those
green eyes
and i was locking
the cage door
myself.

when you ended things you acted like i was the world's
biggest fool. you said to me, "i don't know where you got
the idea that this was anything permanent." the thing is,
you told me a million beautiful things. you told me i was
lovely. you said i was different. so you can't say i was
stupid for thinking it was real. you can't say i was a
complete idiot for believing you when you told me i was
the only one you wanted to be with and that you'd rather
be here with me than anywhere else. you can't say that.

if all of it was fake
you must be the world's best actor
and i must be the
most naive audience member
of all time

-you had me convinced

people who say
it's stupid to cry
over a situationship ending
have simply
never been in one.

some things that just don't make sense if it wasn't real:

the way you would smile softly at me

how you'd compliment the parts of me
nobody had ever noticed before

you laughing at my jokes

the fact that you showed up
when no one else did

how you listened to my late-night thoughts

the way it felt like you really cared

the fact that i fell for you
when you were so romantic
so intentional
with your gestures
says more about your

narcissistic
lying
manipulative
tendencies

than it does
about me

this was just a casual thing
you said over and over
but we both know
this stopped being
fucking *casual*
a long time ago
and you did nothing
to stop it

it was sunny the day you left me
i hope that means
there's still light in my life
somewhere

-even though i can't see it right now

seven months
we made it to seven months

my friends were impressed
they said
*we thought you might've been
the one to make him settle down*

i said
*yeah
i did too*

i would have begged you to stay
if you had given me the chance to

how embarrassing is that?

although
maybe you wanted me to grovel
wanted me on my knees
pleading with you
crying *don't go*
and *please stay*

i guess i'm glad
i still had enough of my pride left
to keep me from doing that

could i have done more?
could i have been more interesting?
what if i had put out more?
what if i had demanded less honesty?
should i have laughed louder?
should i have been sexier?
was it my body?
was it my personality?
how did i lose you?
when did you decide i wasn't enough?
or was i just always

not enough?

-intrusive thoughts

what did i do to make you decide i wasn't worth it?

i was just trying my best

i don't know if another person will ever be able to break
down my walls after you. are you proud of that? does the
fact that i opened up so easily for you but won't be able
to do the same for anyone else make you happy? are you
pleased to have those parts of me and know that no one
else will ever get them? sometimes i feel like that's what
you always planned to do. like my secrets were just a prize
to be won. like my armor was just an obstacle to conquer,
and not what guarded a real, beating heart.

a heart that you fucking broke and walked away from like
you couldn't care less.

maybe one day
i'll forgive you
but right now
i'll just laugh at the idea
of ever giving you
anything resembling
kindness and understanding
again

-you don't deserve it

i loved you more than i loved myself
you wouldn't know what that feels like
so busy only caring about yourself

i can't help but feel like
it was all some big joke

and my heartbreak was the punchline

-well i'm not laughing

music was always there to comfort me. but i showed you all my favorite songs. we'd sing them in the car. i would send you lyrics that reminded me of you, of us. so now it's all tainted with our memories, smeared with the stains of what i thought was love.

i've started preferring the silence.

i know that i'm young
and i've got my whole life
ahead of me
and in a year
or two or three
this won't hurt as much
or maybe even at all

but right now
it does

right now
this is agony

i don't know.
i'm starting to think
that you liked the attention
more than you ever
liked me.

-tough pill to swallow

i'm going to
look back on this
one day
and be glad
it didn't work

but god
tonight
i really wish it did

i am so tired
of giving everything
to people who only
give me fucking crumbs
in return.

is there anybody out there
who can meet me halfway?

isn't there at least one person
who won't take all of me
and leave me starving?

-i just want something equal

one day, you're going to miss me. i know you will. one day, you will realize you wish i was there to laugh at your jokes and comfort you after a bad day. you'll find yourself longing for my soft hands and gentle smile. you'll yearn to hear my voice and taste my skin. and maybe among all of that, it'll hit you that maybe you did love me, after all. but it'll be too late. i won't be around for you to say it to. you'll be stuck with it, and you'll be alone. on that day, you'll realize how good you had it with me, but by then i'll have realized how much better i deserved.

-too little, too late

let's face it
you just got scared

we were too close
for comfort

you were becoming
dependent on me

i was too eager
too vulnerable
too kind

and you liked
all of it too much

we just became
too much

and you ran
because of it

i won't lie:
those first few nights
after you left
were the worst nights
of my entire life

i barely slept
barely ate
barely did anything
except cry

i felt like
a part of me
had gone with you
and i was bleeding
from the hole
left behind

at some point
somebody is going to hurt you
the way you hurt me

and i won't lie—
i'm kind of
looking forward
to that

-*karma*

i think you and i were just fated to break.

-harsh reality

61

if it was meant to be it would have been
if it was meant to be it would have been
if it was meant to be it would have been
if it was meant to be it would have been

-trying to make sense of it all

i'm not the first heart you've broken like this. you've done this countless times before. and i know now those should have been my warning signs. i know i should have realized that their past was going to become my future if i let you in. but it's so nice, thinking you're the exception and not just another part of the rule. it's intoxicating, believing you're the one who's going to change somebody for the better. and i was drunk on it. but i was never going to fix you and your destructive tendencies. i never even stood a chance.

-you can't fix them

i had always known that you were never mine
but it hurts to know that i was only ever yours
in my head

-*delusion*

next time
i'll make sure
to demand the respect
i know i deserve

i won't be the
last resort
or the second
third
fourth
option

i will be
the one
they choose
every day
without hesitation

i don't know
who i'm supposed to
end up with

but i hope
they don't look anything
like you

-i don't want any reminders

i'll forget you
piece by piece
until one day
you'll fade from my mind
completely

and the irony is
i won't even know
i've done something
worth celebrating

-the feat of forgetting

i hate that this was my first taste of love
i hate that you made it so rotten

-*spoiled*

for a while i tried to convince myself that this didn't
count, that i didn't really love you. but it did count. i did
love you. even if it wasn't real for you, it was for me. so it
counts, even if i'm the only one keeping score.

i can proudly say that i don't get it—the need to use
people until you've emptied them of their entire souls.
why would you prefer that over building something real
and meaningful? why would you rather destroy
somebody's trust and scar them forever when you could
bring such beauty and joy into their life?

-i just don't understand it

saw you with a new girl
last week

it's been what,
a month?

i realized i never knew
how long you had waited
before moving on
to me
all those months ago

and if this is
any indication

i don't know why
i ever let myself
believe you'd do anything
other than break my heart

out of curiosity
i asked one of our mutual friends
what happened to you and your new fling
a few weeks later

they said
oh
i don't even think
they're talking anymore

and despite it
i felt a twinge of pride
in my chest

maybe i was different to you
in your own little fucked up way
to have lasted so long
before you got tired of me

i need to feel this
i need to learn this lesson
so i've gotta cry the tears
and scream out the anger
i've gotta make sure
i remember this feeling

so i never find myself
feeling it again

i deserve somebody
who is emotionally capable
of loving me back
and not just a sorry excuse
for it

-so do you

i won't trust somebody again
for a long time
and it'll be even longer
before i let myself
fall in love with someone new

but that's the price i'm willing to pay
to keep my heart safe
from people like you

for weeks i went about my day
more ghost than human
half-present and half-awake
part of me still stuck
in the past
refusing to let go
of the time when
you and i were
together

-i can't let it go

i can't wait
for the day
where i wake up
and don't think of you
at all

i'm sure
i'll get my heart broken
again

but that doesn't seem
as scary to me right now
because it means
i'll have moved on from you

-glass half full

fuck you for making me feel like i wasn't enough
i was and i am
it's not my fault you couldn't see that

i didn't think
i'd ever feel
something for you
stronger than love

then i met grief

it was so much easier to hate you than it was to miss you, so i gave myself over to it. i wrapped my wounded heart up in so much anger and hatred that there wasn't any room left for softness. and for a while, that felt like healing.

until it didn't. it only worked for so long. eventually, i had to feel the pain. i had to feel the sadness alongside the anger. and with that came the agonizing realization that i didn't hate you, not really. despite everything, what i felt for you wasn't true hatred.

it was grief. i was grieving the person i thought you were: a person who loved me, i guess, or at the very least a person who wanted to be with me.

i was having a funeral for something that could have been if you had been a different person. i was mourning a love that simply never was.

loving you left the biggest bruise
i am a dozen shades of purple and blue

they ask me about you
and i laugh

oh, him?
i say
he was nothing
just a fling
that got a bit messy
that's all

-a dream that hasn't come true yet

i still wish it could have been different
but i am learning to be glad that it wasn't

if commitment is what you want
don't ever accept anything less
sacrificing your standards
will not make you happy

-take it from me

i'm staying true to myself next time
and trusting my damn gut
i've had a strong intuition my whole life
and it screamed when i met you
i learned too late that i should've fucking listened

-*listen to your gut*

and suddenly,
the thought of you
doesn't make me ache
anymore

i've never been
so happy to feel
nothing at all

-numb to you

i've grown enough to say
that i hope you're happy
even if that's not with me

and i especially hope
you're in fucking therapy

-you need it

met you in the summer
and we started off hot
fell for you in autumn
alongside the leaves
you left me in the winter
cold and bitter
now spring is here
just in time for me
to bloom anew

i have always been enough
i just have to make sure
i surround myself with
the people who know that

not every person is going to belong in my life
i have to learn to be okay with that

at the end of it
you were just some boy
who wasn't worth my time
or my tears

-sadly i gave you both of them

everybody's life is a giant jigsaw puzzle
and people either fit into a place
or they don't

i refuse to make anybody stay with me
if they don't want to

if they wish to leave
i'll hold the door open for them
myself

i look back on who i was all those months ago and i want
to cringe. i want to laugh, and say she was so pathetic. but
i love her still. i know she was doing the best she could.
she didn't know what i know now. she couldn't have. it's
how she ended up in that mess in the first place.

-hindsight

you are worth so much more than the bare minimum

someday i hope you see me again
when i'm in love with someone new

and i hope you look at all the love there
and think about how you almost had it
it was right in front of you and you let it
slip
    right
        through
            your
                fingers

i pieced myself back together
and i don't give a fuck
if you can't recognize me
through all the patchwork

i'm not looking for anybody
to fall in love with right now
i'm content to be by myself
because if there's one person
who can be trusted with my heart
it's me

i genuinely believe
that what happened
was for the best

even if we'd lasted
longer than we did
the ending
was never
going to be
any different

better to have
lost you after months
instead of years

sometimes
i check your instagram
just to see what you've been up to

you are so laughably the same
while i feel like a brand new person

-heartbreak does that to you

i am resolved
to never
ever
let somebody
walk all over me
like you did
again.

the biggest challenge
i've faced isn't getting over you
it's learning how to
set my own boundaries
and stick to them

i'm done putting
my effort into
people who
aren't interested
in all that
i can give them

if you don't want all of me
you don't get a single piece

maybe one day you'll stop letting your cowardice win

105

i hope you figure your shit out
and learn how to be kind to people
who only want what's best for you

-what i wish for you

i also hope you realize
life is so much more beautiful
if you open yourself up to love

-what i wish for you, part two

finally, i hope you find somebody
who makes you want to stick around
even, or maybe especially, if it's not me

-what i wish for you, part three

i can't quite say it yet
but one day i'll forgive you
i know that's where i'm headed
and i can't wait to get there

-the last battle

my heart bears its scars quite proudly
they are proof of my courage to dare to fall in love

took all the love
i could've given you
if you'd let me
and put it into other things:

my home
my friends
my family
my dreams
myself

all those tears i cried over you
nurtured some beautiful seeds
i'm surrounded by a garden now
and i'm filled with love—for me

i'm not done healing
but one day
i'm gonna get there

-one step at a time

i'm grateful you showed me what i didn't want in a relationship. even if it hurt. even if it ripped me to pieces. because now i know my own worth. now i know what it is i deserve. and that's better than what you could have ever given me. it always was.

i see now
that not being meant
to be with somebody
is a blessing

you'll be glad for it
in the end

there is so much
love out there
that's destined to be

yours

thank you for reading! i hope you enjoyed my book.
please consider leaving a review on amazon if you did!

fated to break · olive rhodes